JAMES A. GARFIELD

ENCYCLOPEDIA
of PRESIDENTS

James A. Garfield

Twentieth President of the United States

By Dee Lillegard

Consultant: Charles Abele, Ph.D.
Social Studies Instructor
Chicago Public School System

CHILDRENS PRESS ®

CHICAGO

JB
Garfield

GARFIELD MONUMENT

FUND.

ELIZA BALLOU GARFIELD

LUCRETIA RUDOLPH GARFIELD

BORN NOV. 19 TH 1831

DIED SEPT 19 TH 1881

This Certifies that *Huldah H. Robertson* has contributed *Two Dollars* to the fund for the erection of a monument in *Lake View Cemetery* to the memory of

J. A. Garfield

LATE PRESIDENT OF THE UNITED STATES.

Cleveland, O.

Committee

A certificate for a contribution to the Garfield Monument Fund.
Garfield is shown flanked by his mother and his wife.

Dedication: For Collin Quincy, who memorized the presidents when he was seven

Library of Congress Cataloging-in-Publication Data

Lillegard, Dee.
   James A. Garfield.

   (Encyclopedia of presidents)
   Includes index.
   Summary: A biography of the twentieth president of
the United States, the last President to be born in a
log cabin.
   1.   Garfield, James A. (James Abram), 1831-1881 —
Juvenile literature.   2.   Presidents—United States—
Biography—Juvenile literature.   [1.   Garfield, James A.
(James Abram), 1831-1881.   2.   Presidents]   I.   Title.
II.   Series.
E687.L55   1987   973.8'4'0924 [B] [92]   87-18200
ISBN 0-516-01394-7

PHb

Picture Acknowledgments

Historical Pictures Service—4, 5, 6, 8 (top), 9
(top), 12, 17, 19 (top), 22, 24, 26, 27 (bottom),
30, 32, 34, 35, 36, 37, 38, 39 (top), 41, 46, 49,
51, 55 (top right, bottom), 56, 63 (bottom), 64,
66, 67 (2 pictures), 70, 72, 73, 75 (2 pictures),
80, 82, 83, 85 (top)

Courtesy Library of Congress—14, 16, 19
(bottom), 23, 31, 40 (bottom), 43, 54

North Wind Picture Archives—8 (bottom), 9
(bottom), 10, 11, 20, 21, 27 (top), 28, 29, 33
(2 pictures), 39 (bottom), 40 (top), 42, 44, 47,
48, 52, 53 (2 pictures), 55 (top left), 58, 60, 61,
62, 63 (top), 65 (2 pictures), 68, 76, 77, 78, 81,
84, 85 (bottom), 86, 87, 88, 89

U.S. Bureau of Printing and Engraving—2, 13

Cover design and illustration by
Steven Gaston Dobson

A relief sculpture for the Garfield monument in Cleveland, Ohio, showing Garfield taking the presidential oath. The sculptor was Caspar Buberl.

Table of Contents

Chapter 1

A Rising Star

It was late 1859 when the newly elected state senator arrived by train at Columbus, the capital of Ohio. He was a big, strong, spirited young man with striking blue eyes and light curling hair and whiskers. He liked to throw an arm around a friend's shoulders while he was talking.

The energetic Senator James A. Garfield was always ready for a debate. He had a pleasant baritone voice and made speeches on every measure that came before the Ohio senate. He even spoke against a bill to tax dogs—all dogs, that is, except "ladies' poodles."

On more serious issues, Garfield vigorously defended the state of Ohio from any involvement in John Brown's raid on Harper's Ferry, Virginia. A federal arsenal was located at Harper's Ferry, and John Brown and his followers planned to take guns from it to arm the slaves in the South. The raiders struck from southern Ohio, crossing the border to attack the arsenal, but failed to capture it. Outraged by Brown's attempt, southerners blamed Ohio, their northern neighbor. Garfield insisted the state could not be held responsible for what a handful of fanatics had done on their own.

Opposite page: James Garfield
as a representative from Ohio

Left: John Brown, the
abolitionist who led the
raid on Harper's Ferry

Below: A view from Loudon
Heights, Virginia, showing
Harper's Ferry in the valley

Above: The capture of John Brown at Harper's Ferry

Right: John Brown on the way to his execution

Industry flourished in the North in the 1850s.

The incident dramatized the dangerous gulf widening between the North and the South in the late 1850s. At that time the South was almost totally rural, whereas the North boasted many thriving cities and urban areas. The South had little manufacturing, while industry flourished in the North. The South would have welcomed the many immigrants who poured into the country from Europe. Instead, the immigrants settled in the North and West because they did not care to compete with slave labor.

The South's economy depended on the labor of black slaves.

Slavery remained the most serious problem between the two sections of the country. The South feared that its slave labor system would be disrupted by the North, and the North feared that radical southerners would try to spread slavery throughout the nation. Despite efforts to work out a compromise between the two regions, many people believed a civil war was fast approaching.

The city of Cincinnati, Ohio, around 1860

Emotions ran high in June of 1860 when Garfield addressed the state Republican convention. His speech, according to a Cincinnati newspaper, brought him "at once . . . into genuine popularity as a political speaker."

"Your praise is on everyone's mouth," a friend wrote to Garfield. Suddenly he found himself overwhelmed by requests to speak all over the state.

The young senator described his summer as a "whirlpool of excitement and work." Garfield spoke for the Republican candidate for president at over forty meetings and had to turn down at least that many more invitations. The newspapers described him as "a rising man."

When the Republican candidate, Abraham Lincoln, won the election, Garfield rejoiced. He described Lincoln as "thoroughly honest." Lincoln's "remarkable good sense," Garfield went on, "gives me great hopes for the country."

President Abraham Lincoln

In the next few years, however, Garfield would oppose many of the president's policies, nor would he be so enthusiastic in 1864 at Lincoln's reelection. Yet his opposition to Lincoln did not affect his appreciation of the man. In April 1865, on hearing the news of Lincoln's assassination—his fatal wound from a pistol fired at the back of his head—Garfield would write: "My heart is so broken with our great national loss that I can hardly think or write or speak. . . . I am sick at heart."

He could not know then that a similar fate awaited him as the future twentieth president. For now, Garfield's star was rapidly rising.

The birthplace of James Abram Garfield in Orange township, Ohio

Chapter 2

Canal Boy

James A. Garfield, born November 19, 1831, was the last of the presidents to be born in a log cabin. His mother remembered him as "the largest Babe I ever had."

Eliza Garfield named her new son James Abram in memory of another son with the same name, who had died at two years of age. Before the second James Abram turned two, his father—Abram Garfield—died. Eliza was left with four children to raise. Three of them were able to help the Widow Garfield farm her land in Orange township, Ohio (now Moreland Hills). But baby James, her favorite, was too young to work. A bright and active boy, little Jim grew up as the family pet.

Garfield's birthplace was located a few miles south of Cleveland in the northern part of Ohio known as the Western Reserve. It was mostly wilderness at the time, and Cleveland—soon to be a much larger city—barely had a thousand inhabitants. A friend would later say of Garfield, "to the very last it was apparent that he was country-born." There was something in "his voice, his dress, his walk, his ways" that suggested "woods and fields rather than drawing rooms."

The schoolhouse where James Garfield attended school

When Jim was three years old, his sister Hitty began carrying him through the woods to the little red district schoolhouse. It was a six-mile round trip on foot. Before long, Jim was reading from the family Bible.

Eliza decided that the township of Orange should have a school of its own. She offered a corner of her land for it, and neighbors built a crude log schoolhouse there. Now Jim could go to school and be close enough to home to help with farm chores.

For much of his childhood, Garfield lived alone with his mother and a sister, Mary, who was seven years older than he. It is said that he "ruled the house" and that by the age of eight was running wild. In later years, Garfield described his childhood as "chaos" and wished he had had more discipline and guidance.

James Garfield
at the age of
sixteen years

Young Garfield was not very handy on the farm. Lost in a private dream world, he would absentmindedly slash himself with an axe while chopping wood. He loved to read, and frequent illnesses gave him many opportunities to read—and reread—his favorite books. Stories of the sea fascinated him most of all. Whenever Jim had a free afternoon, he would hang around the wharves of Cleveland and run errands for the canal boat captains. Their tales of adventure in faraway places thrilled him.

At one point Jim, who was left-handed, began to keep a journal. He wrote in it that he enjoyed school. He was eager to get on with his life, however. By the age of sixteen he had become handy enough to earn good wages and often had jobs that took him away from the farm.

In the summer of 1848, young Garfield left home to go to sea. He headed straight for the now-bustling port of Cleveland.

When a half-drunk captain refused to take Garfield on his ship, Jim turned instead to the Ohio and Pennsylvania Canal. There he got a job prodding the dray horses that slowly pulled the barges. He fell into the canal fourteen times! Since he could not swim, he had to be fished out each time.

Even though Garfield was promoted to better jobs on the canal, after six weeks he fell ill and had to return home. He lay in bed, feverish, from October 1848 until January 1849. His mother took care of him and convinced him not to go back to the canal. Even a sailor, she said, needs an education.

Garfield then enrolled at a Baptist school called the Geauga Academy in nearby Chester township. Most of the students at Geauga had a limited education, and their teachers were not far ahead of them. After eight months at the academy, Garfield himself received a certificate to teach school, although he was still a student.

Jobs as a carpenter and then as a teacher helped Garfield support himself at Geauga. The pay was low, and one whole spring term he had to survive on only milk, bread, and pudding.

As a boy, James had felt humiliated to be poor and to be known as "Widow Garfield's Jimmie." Now he felt humiliated by his coarse, homemade clothes—a faded wool shirt and patched trousers—and by the snubs of the bet-ter-dressed students.

Above: A young boy leading horses as they tow canal barges
Below: A view of Harper's Ferry

The country school where James Garfield was a teacher

Garfield left Geauga to earn money so that he could continue his education more comfortably. He got a job teaching at a country school, where he proved his qualifications by beating the local bully who had driven away the last teacher.

Having become a member of a church called the Disciples of Christ, Garfield decided to continue his education at their school in Hiram, Ohio. There, at the Western Reserve Eclectic School (later named Hiram College), he supported himself as a student by working as a janitor. No one snubbed Garfield at the Eclectic. He impressed both teachers and students with his scholastic ability, as well as with his size—he was six feet tall with broad shoulders, and he could outrun and outwrestle his schoolmates.

Hiram College, formerly called Western Reserve Eclectic School

At the Eclectic, Garfield discovered that he had the power to sway an audience; he was a natural speaker. He also discovered Lucretia ("Crete") Rudolph, the daughter of one of the school's trustees and his future bride.

After three years at Hiram, Garfield attended Williams College in Williamstown, Massachusetts. One winter he taught school at North Pownal, Vermont, replacing Chester A. Arthur. Ironically, Arthur, the previous teacher, would one day succeed Garfield as president of the United States.

Williams College in Williamstown, Massachusetts

In 1856 Garfield graduated from Williams with honors. He returned to Hiram College and was appointed professor of Latin and Greek. The following year, at the age of twenty-six, he was made president of the school. In the spring of 1858, after a long engagement, he and Crete were married.

In 1859 Garfield, restless and dissatisfied with his work, began to study law on his own. That same year, the opportunity arose for him to run for a seat in the state

Lucretia Rudolph Garfield

senate. He had made a name for himself preaching, lecturing, and publicly debating issues of the day. Locally, he was a well-known and well-respected Republican. He stood a good chance of becoming state senator.

In all of his campaign speeches, Garfield cried out against slavery and praised the Republicans as champions of free labor. His victory was a turning point in his life. Politics—not teaching, preaching, or the law—was to be James A. Garfield's career.

The Battle of Corinth during the American Civil War

Chapter 3

Civil War

At the age of twenty-eight, Garfield was the youngest member of the Ohio legislature. He had a lot to learn about "the run of Legislative business." Luckily he shared a room in Columbus with another legislator, whose experience was a great help to him.

Shortly after Garfield made his popular speech at the Ohio Republican convention, he and Crete became parents of a daughter, Eliza. Although Garfield loved his growing family, he had to be away from Crete and Eliza many times during the campaign of 1860. The party needed his skills as a speaker to help Lincoln win the presidential campaign.

Lincoln's election in November led some of the southern states to secede, or withdraw, from the Union. To these states, Lincoln represented a party that was against southern interests. In the four months following the election, seven slave states in the Deep South voted to secede. They formed a new nation, the Confederate States of America, and chose Jefferson Davis to be the first president of their Confederacy.

President James Buchanan

The southern states, as they seceded, took possession of federal properties within their borders. South Carolina, however, could not immediately seize Fort Sumter in Charleston harbor. President Buchanan, in the last days of his term, refused to give up the fort. When he tried to strengthen it with fresh troops and supplies, South Carolina's military forces fired on the unarmed supply ship that Buchanan had sent. The prospect of war seemed unavoidable.

Above: Jefferson Davis, president of the Confederate States of America
Below: Jefferson Davis with his cabinet

HARPER'S WEEKLY.

A JOURNAL OF CIVILIZATION.

VOL. IV.—No. 208.]   NEW YORK, SATURDAY, DECEMBER 22, 1860.   [PRICE FIVE CENTS.

Entered according to Act of Congress, in the Year 1860, by Harper & Brothers, in the Clerk's Office of the District Court for the Southern District of New York.

KEITT.
BOYCE.   CHESNUT.   M'QUEEN.
ASHMORE.   HAMMOND.   BONHAM.
MILES.

THE SECEDING SOUTH CAROLINA DELEGATION.—[PHOTOGRAPHED BY BRADY.]

Above: An 1860 cartoon showing the evils of secession
Opposite page: Representatives from the seceding state of South Carolina

HON. ABRAHAM LINCOLN, OF ILLINOIS.   HON. HANNIBAL HAMLIN, OF MAINE,

FOR PRESIDENT.   FOR VICE PRESIDENT.

The inauguration of Abraham Lincoln at the Capitol, March 4, 1861

Lincoln took office in March 1861. He soon made it clear that he regarded the secession as illegal and that he would not let the seceded states take federal property. He urged the Confederate states to return to the Union. By April, the troops at Fort Sumter—nearly out of provisions—were starving. Lincoln informed South Carolina that he was sending another unarmed ship with supplies.

The Confederates decided to attack Fort Sumter. They felt that it should belong to them, not to the Union from which they had withdrawn. After thirty-four hours of steady bombardment, the helpless fort surrendered to the Confederacy. The country was at war.

Opposite page: A Republican campaign banner for the election of 1860

Union soldiers loading a cannon to defend Fort Sumter

Garfield wrote to a friend of his feelings about this Union defeat: "I am glad we are defeated at Sumter. It will rouse the people [of the North]. . . . The war will soon assume the shape of Slavery vs. Freedom."

Many northerners felt this way—that the Union should vigorously fight against both slavery and secession. They had not yet tasted the bitterness of war. In the South, four more states seceded, joining the Confederacy.

Above: Fort Sumter's flag, shot full of holes
Below: Fort Sumter after the Confederates bombarded it

A Civil War recruiting station in New York City Hall

The Union did not have an army ready to fight a war. After Fort Sumter, Lincoln called on the individual states that remained in the Union for 75,000 volunteers.

As the prospect of war was drawing closer, Garfield had begun to read books on military science. Once the fighting began, he volunteered for military service. He was appointed lieutenant colonel, then colonel, of a regiment that did not yet exist—the Forty-Second Ohio Volunteer Regiment.

Volunteers sign up for duty in response to Lincoln's call for recruits.

Garfield spoke at the church in Hiram, urging its young men to fight for their country. Sixty of them immediately stepped forward to join the Forty-Second. By the end of the day, Hiram College was drained of its students.

Once again, Garfield found himself in a position where he had much to learn and little time to waste. But he had been a good teacher, and he was used to disciplining students. Even though he lacked military experience, he had the natural abilities of a leader.

A great bridge of boats, a mile in length, built by the Union forces
across the Ohio River to the Illinois shore

In late 1861, Garfield was given command of the Eighteenth Brigade, three thousand men divided into four
regiments—including the Forty-Second—plus cavalry.
His task was to drive Confederate forces out of eastern
Kentucky, which seemed a huge responsibility to him. He
soon found himself in a mountainous region where winter
weather was harsh, and the roads were channels of half-
frozen mud. The Confederates, who outnumbered Garfield's troops, lay hidden among trees and rocks.

Garfield's first battle left him shaken. "It was a terrible
sight," he wrote to his mother, "to walk over the battle

A Cincinnati regiment building a road across Low Island in the Ohio River, across from Paducah, Kentucky

field and see the horrible faces of the dead rebels stretched on the hill in all shapes and positions." The innocent teacher and budding politician would never be the same.

Garfield and his brigade were successful in driving the Confederates out of Kentucky, with few casualties on their side. But foul weather and an epidemic caused more losses to the brigade than the fighting. After over fifty young men from Ohio died of illness in Kentucky, Garfield wrote: "This fighting with disease is infinitely more horrible than battle." And, he added, he would not want to have to face the fathers of the boys he had so enthusiastically enlisted.

Brigadier General James Garfield

For his success, Garfield was made a brigadier general at the age of thirty. With regret he left the young men of his Forty-Second regiment and moved on to Shiloh and Corinth, on either side of the Tennessee and Mississippi borders. The Union forces—under General Ulysses S. Grant—had just been badly beaten in this area. Further battles only brought Garfield more "horrible sights." "No blaze of glory," he wrote, could ever make up for the "unutterable horrors" of war.

Above: The Battle of Shiloh
Below: After the Battle of Corinth

Left: Brigadier General
Ulysses S. Grant

Below: Abraham Lincoln
visits the headquarters
of the Army of the Potomac
on October 4, 1862.

Major General William S. Rosecrans

In 1863 Garfield became chief of staff to Major General William Rosecrans. He distinguished himself at the battle of Chickamauga in September when, even though his horse was shot from under him, he safely delivered a message that saved the army of the Cumberland from disaster. For his bravery, he was promoted to major general.

From this time on, Crete would always refer to her husband as "General Garfield." During the war months, she managed to save enough money to buy their own home in Hiram.

Congressmen assembled in the House of Representatives in the 1860s

While on active duty in 1862, Garfield had been elected to the United States House of Representatives, but his term would not begin until December 1863. While in Washington, he told President Lincoln that he did not want to leave the army. Lincoln convinced Garfield that the administration needed a soldier in Congress, someone who understood the army's needs. So at Lincoln's urging, Garfield agreed to take his seat in the House.

Garfield wearing a hat

In November, Garfield returned to Hiram to be with Crete, their daughter Eliza, and new son Harry before his congressional term began. But three-year-old "Trot," as Garfield had nicknamed his daughter, became ill. On December 1, 1863, he wrote to a friend: "Our darling Trot died at 7 o'clock this evening . . . how desolate our hearts are tonight."

It was a sad and lonely Garfield who joined the U.S. Congress. He could not imagine what lay before him.

Congressman Garfield

Chapter 4

Congressman Garfield

The members of this session of Congress were the first to be elected in wartime. They found themselves in a difficult position. The Civil War overshadowed all other issues, and there were many empty seats on the Democratic side of the House—seats left by representatives of the seceded states.

Most congressmen did not bring their families to Washington, and Garfield found a place to live in one of the boardinghouses typical of the time. He was lonely without his family and still grieving the loss of his little Trot. Finally setting aside his general's uniform on December 6, 1863, he took the congressional seat that he would occupy for the next seventeen years.

The Capitol building was a disappointment to visitors in 1863. Its unswept tile floors were littered with apple cores and stained with tobacco juice. The south wing belonged to the House of Representatives, and the "Hall of the House" was poorly lit and overheated. Garfield complained, "Any man sitting here, during the evening, can feel his skull and brain going through the slow process of roasting."

The Capitol in 1863, with its unfinished dome

The members of Congress had no offices of their own and conducted their business from their congressional seats. They paid little attention to those who tried to speak. Garfield, though the youngest member of the House, was one of the few who could get their attention and keep it. He quickly earned respect for his speaking ability.

His military experience also brought Garfield respect, as well as a position on the Military Affairs Committee. He worked hard for legislation that would help Lincoln maintain the Union army.

Garfield was one of the few congressmen who could find his way around the Library of Congress. It was said that he used its books more than any other legislator. He once confessed to a friend: "Not a week passes in which I do not long to be . . . engaged again in study and teaching."

President Lincoln leaving Jefferson Davis's mansion

In December 1863, at the beginning of the first session of the Thirty-Eighth Congress, Lincoln announced his plan for Reconstruction of the South. Eleven states had seceded from the Union. How should they be treated when the Civil War was over? How was the Union to be rebuilt?

Reconstruction was a subject on which the Republicans strongly disagreed. Garfield was among those who felt that Lincoln was too softhearted and would be too generous to the South when the war was over. He called for harsher measures than Lincoln proposed. Later he would say, "I am a poor hater," and would soften his own views.

Ulysses S. Grant with Massachusetts volunteers, surveying the Confederates' position

In March 1864, General Ulysses S. Grant took supreme command of all the Union armies. This meant that the Union forces, which had been divided in their efforts, were now cooperating as a strong, single force. A Union victory seemed certain, and the question of Reconstruction grew more heated.

In November 1864 Lincoln was reelected, and in December Garfield returned to Washington for the second session of the Thirty-Eighth Congress. He rented rooms for his family, and from then on they would live with him whenever he was in Washington.

Generals Robert E. Lee and Ulysses S. Grant sign the surrender at Appomattox, April 9, 1865.

The end of the war was clearly in sight, and Garfield's work on the Military Affairs Committee lost much of its urgency. To prepare for the coming problems of peacetime, Garfield began to study financial questions. He was soon to become the most knowledgeable congressman on the subject of finance and the economy.

In the spring of 1865, the South surrendered to the Union. Now the period of Reconstruction began. It was the beginning of a new era in the history of the United States.

The ruins of Columbia, South Carolina, after General William Sherman destroyed it on his march to the sea in February 1865

The South lay in ruins. Thousands of white refugees wandered over its wasted lands. The four million blacks who were free at last were unsure of what the future held for them.

Should the freed slaves have full civil rights immediately, including the right to vote? Who should decide—the federal government or the southern states? Although Garfield was in favor of allowing the freed slaves to vote, many people did not believe that they should. Most freed slaves, they argued, could not read or write and had no education.

The Pinckney residence, a colonial mansion in Charleston, South Carolina, after the war

Black slaves joyfully leaving their fields
as they hear of the Union victory

Garfield insisted that the former slaves were no different than the European immigrants who were pouring into the country once again now that the war was over. Most of these immigrants could not speak English. If an education test were to be given to voters, Garfield said, "let it apply to all alike." The color of a person's skin should not be the basis of suffrage.

How should the North handle the defeated southern states? Should they be brought back into the Union with full states' rights? Many northerners, including Garfield, were against this.

Above: Freed slaves crossing into northern territory
Below: Freedom—the old style and the new

The assassination of Abraham Lincoln at Ford's Theatre on April 14, 1865

On April 14, 1865, Lincoln argued again for generous treatment of the South. His assassination that evening at Ford's Theatre in Washington shocked and enraged northerners. They blamed the South for what the assassin, John Wilkes Booth, had done.

The new president, Andrew Johnson, tried to carry on where Lincoln had left off; but he soon found himself battling Congress. Johnson needed someone who could act as a mediator between himself and the angry legislators. James Garfield seemed to be the right man.

War Department, Washington, April 20, 1865.

$100,000 REWARD!
THE MURDERER
Of our late beloved President, ABRAHAM LINCOLN,
IS STILL AT LARGE.
$50,000 REWARD!
will be paid by this Department for his apprehension, in addition to any reward offered by Municipal Authorities or State Executives.
$25,000 REWARD!
will be paid for the apprehension of JOHN H. SURRATT, one of Booth's accomplices.
$25,000 REWARD!
will be paid for the apprehension of DANIEL C. HARROLD, another of Booth's accomplices.

LIBERAL REWARDS will be paid for any information that shall conduce to the arrest of either of the above-named criminals, or their accomplices.

All persons harboring or secreting the said persons, or either of them, or aiding or assisting their concealment or escape, will be treated as accomplices in the murder of the President and the attempted assassination of the Secretary of State, and shall be subject to trial before a Military Commission and the punishment of DEATH.

Let the stain of innocent blood be removed from the land by the arrest and punishment of the murderers.

All good citizens are exhorted to aid public justice on this occasion. Every man should consider his own conscience charged with this solemn duty, and rest neither night nor day until it be accomplished.

EDWIN M. STANTON, *Secretary of War.*

DESCRIPTIONS.—BOOTH is 5 feet 7 or 8 inches high, slender build, high forehead, black hair, black eyes, and wears a heavy black moustache.
JOHN H. SURRATT is about 5 feet 9 inches. Hair rather thin and dark, eyes rather light, no beard. Would weigh 145 or 150 pounds. Complexion rather pale and clear, with color in his cheeks. Wore light clothes of fine quality. Shoulders square, cheek bones rather prominent, chin narrow, ears projecting at the top, forehead rather low and square, but broad. Parts his hair on the right side; neck rather long. His lips are firmly set. A slim man.
DANIEL C. HARROLD is 22 years of age; 5 feet 6 or 7 inches high, rather broad shouldered, glancesly light build, dark hair little of any; moustache. Dark eyes, weighs about 140 pounds.

GEO. F. NESBITT & CO., Printers and Stationers, cor. Pearl and Pine Streets, N. Y.

Above: A poster issued by the U.S. secretary of war, announcing rewards for the capture of Booth and his accomplices

Above right: John Wilkes Booth

Below right: Andrew Johnson, who succeeded Abraham Lincoln as president

Chapter 5

Mr. Chairman

In the beginning, Garfield had hopes of cooperating with President Johnson. "Some foolish men among us," he wrote, "are all the while bristling up for a fight and seem to be anxious to make a rupture with Johnson. I think we should assume that he is with us, treat him kindly, without suspicion, and go on in a firm, calmly considered course."

But "calmness" was not possible in the emotional postwar climate. And Johnson's rash personality and bad temper did not help matters.

In April 1866, Garfield voted in favor of the Civil Rights Act (giving citizenship to blacks) over President Johnson's veto. Feelings against the president grew so strong that congressmen wanted to impeach him. In December 1867, Garfield voted against a resolution to do so. But on February 22, 1868, he voted with other Republicans for impeachment, and Johnson came within one vote of losing his office. Nine months later, General Ulysses S. Grant was elected to the presidency. Garfield, though he supported Grant, would find himself once again in an uncomfortable relationship with the chief executive.

A cartoon reflecting the country's growing dislike of President Andrew Johnson

Altogether, Garfield was to be elected to Congress eight times in a row. By 1869, his seat in Congress seemed so secure that he decided to buy a home in Washington. For five years, during congressional sessions, he had been dragging his growing family from one set of furnished rooms to another. Now there would be two homes—a three-story red brick house in Washington and the smaller house in Hiram, Ohio.

In January 1869, Garfield was sworn into his seat in Congress. He was appointed to the Committee on Banking and Currency and was made its chairman. He was also chairman of the Select Committee on the Census. Garfield urged that the census be broadened into a great fact-gathering agency that would provide information valuable to lawmakers. His recommendations were not accepted at the time, but ten years later many were included in the planning of the 1880 census. For this reason, Garfield has been called the "father of the modern census."

In December 1871, Garfield was put in charge of the Appropriations Committee, which was responsible for government monies. Before this time, appropriations—or monies set aside for various purposes—were scandalously abused. During his four years as chairman of the committee, Garfield studied what things cost. He tried to determine what funds were necessary for every government project. He inspected hospitals, office buildings, telegraphs, schools for the deaf and dumb. "No wheel, no shaft, no rivet in our governmental machinery performs its function without money," he told a friend. He felt he had to know "where every dollar goes and how it is used."

President Grant finds the Republican party crumbling beneath him. Liberals point out that, with them missing, the entire party will collapse.

Garfield worked up to fifteen hours a day for months on end. On some days he had to speak more than forty times to try to get his bills through the House. This experience would give him a greater knowledge of the inner workings of the government than any of the presidents had before him. Before the four years had passed, Garfield would become a highly respected congressman and one of the acknowledged leaders of his party.

Garfield had fears about the future of the Republican party, however. "The war," he observed, "has brought to the surface of National politics many men who are neither fitted in character, nor ability, to be leaders of public thought or representative of the true men of the country."

A cartoonist's view of Grant trying to pass a civil service examination

Garfield did not include President Grant among these men, but he was disappointed to see Grant surrounding himself with such "spoilsmen."

Under the "spoils system," the winning party could give public offices to its supporters. Under Grant, the spoils system became a national disgrace. As a congressman, Garfield had discovered that office seekers "infest every public place . . . meet you at every corner, and thrust their papers in your face as a highwayman would his pistol." Finding government jobs for these people was, he groaned, "the most intolerable burden I have to bear."

By 1870, Garfield had become a champion of civil service reform. There had to be better laws governing the selection of government workers.

Bleached bones on the Western plains

Garfield was so confident of his reelection in 1872 that he did not bother to campaign. He had gained an appointment as commissioner to negotiate with the Flathead Indians in Montana and happily set out to see the West. Although he and Crete had sailed to Europe in the summer of 1867, he had never been beyond the Mississippi River on his own continent.

Garfield sat glued to the window as the train rolled across the Kansas prairie. The ocean of grass was littered with bleached buffalo bones. The Wild West was already a legend—three years before, on May 10, 1869, the first transcontinental railroad had been completed.

Above: The Colorado Mountains.   Below: Union Pacific and Central Pacific engines meet as the "golden spike" is driven in to complete the trancontinental railroad.

Mormon leader Brigham Young

In Salt Lake City, Utah, Garfield chatted with Brigham Young and other leaders of the Mormon church. At Ogden, he left the comfort of the train to ride a stagecoach. He was thrilled to sit up front with the drivers and to sleep in the wilderness on a buffalo robe. As they drove past the Rocky Mountains, Congressman Garfield saw the mountain that had been named in his honor—Mount Garfield, a snow-covered peak on the continental divide.

Garfield was successful in his negotiations with the Indians, persuading the Flatheads to relocate to another reservation. On his way back home, he read an item in the newspaper that disturbed him. "I find my own name dragged into some story which I do not understand," he wrote in his diary.

Above: Indian chiefs meet with government officials at the White House in 1871.
Below: President Grant signs the Force Bill, aimed at controlling the Ku Klux Klan.

No. 486

Originated in the House of Representatives

W. B. Benedict
Clerk of the House of Reps.

An Act to change the name of the Pennsylvania Fiscal Agency

Received March 23 1864.
Approved March 26 1864.
Pay $10.
Paid by Jacob Ziegler Esq into the State Treasury
March 28 1864

An Act to change the name of the Pennsylvania Fiscal Agency.

Section 1. Be it enacted by the Senate and House of Representatives of the Commonwealth of Pennsylvania in General Assembly met and it is hereby enacted by the authority of the same, That from and after the passage of this Act The Pennsylvania Fiscal Agency shall be named instead thereof The Credit Mobilier of America with all the powers privileges and authorities they had under their former name and be subject to all the restrictions and liabilities to which they were subject to under the same

Henry C. Johnson
Speaker of the House of Reps.

John P. Penny
Speaker of the Senate

Approved the 26 day of March Anno Domini One thousand eight hundred and sixty-four

A. G. Curtin

The next election for Garfield was to be his most difficult. The newspapers had said he was involved in a scandal. Garfield was accused of taking bribes from a fellow congressman for stock in a railroad construction company called Crédit Mobilier. Although Garfield was eventually cleared of the charges, the experience was painful for him. His name remained connected in people's minds with the political corruption that existed in the "Gilded Age," the years after the Civil War.

In 1874, the country was in the midst of a depression that was to last for five more years. The people blamed the Republicans, the party in power, for their hard times, and many Republicans lost their seats in Congress. In spite of the problems Garfield had to face, he was one of the small band of survivors. He proved himself to be an able vote-getter and a leader of the party. Two years later he would find himself in the position of "president-maker."

Above: This cartoon published in 1880, the year Garfield ran for president, shows him still burdened with the Crédit Mobilier scandal.

Right: A photograph of James Garfield

Opposite page: The certificate marking the birth of the Crédit Mobilier, a company that was formerly named the Pennsylvania Fiscal Agency

JAMES A. GARFIELD.

Chapter 6

Stalwarts versus Half-Breeds

"The people have gone crazy," Garfield sadly declared. Although victorious in the election of 1874, he was returning to a Congress that would be controlled by Democrats for the rest of his congressional career. As a Republican, he would never again be given command of a committee. He would have to make his mark as a leader of the minority party.

Relieved of committee responsibilities, Garfield decided to take a trip to California. It was something he had wanted to do for years. Crete stayed behind to look after the children: Harry, age eleven; Jimmy, nine; Mollie, eight; and two younger boys, Irvin and Abram.

Garfield, ever the teacher, turned the letters he wrote home into history and geography lessons. He gave his older children puzzles to solve: "When I went to bed it was just 12 o'clock at night by Toledo [Ohio] time, but it was 12:28 by my watch, which is Washington time." The children had to figure out "how many degrees west of Washington" their father was on April 19, 1875. (At that time, each town set its own time by the position of the sun.)

Opposite page: Garfield as the
Republican presidential candidate

James G. Blaine

Three years before, Garfield had gotten as far west as Montana. Now he reached the Pacific coast, visiting San Francisco and Oakland in northern California, then heading south to Los Angeles. He was awed by the Yosemite Valley in California and amazed by the mining "boom towns" of Virginia City and Carson City in Nevada.

Garfield's return to Congress was less than happy. The Grant administration, in its second term, was staggering from scandal to scandal. Yet there were many Republicans, led by New York Senator Roscoe Conkling, who wanted Grant to run for a third term. Garfield sided with other Republicans who preferred James G. Blaine, the senator from Maine, as the presidential candidate for 1876. There were also rumors that Governor Rutherford B. Hayes of Ohio was gaining strength as a candidate.

When Blaine was charged with using his political power for personal gain, his supporters decided that he was too risky a candidate. Garfield, among them, threw his support to Hayes, who won the Republican nomination. Hayes ran against the Democratic candidate, Samuel Tilden, in what was to prove a hotly disputed election.

Garfield won his congressional seat once again, but his happiness was short-lived. While delivering a speech in New Jersey, he received a telegram—his new son Edward, nicknamed Neddy, was very sick.

Shortly after he reached home, the baby died of whooping cough. His heart heavy with sorrow, he watched his last-born child laid to rest on Hiram Hill, next to his firstborn, little Trot.

Further cause for gloom was Hayes's apparent loss to Tilden, who received a quarter of a million more popular votes. But it was the electoral votes that counted—the votes of the presidential electors chosen by the people's votes. And the votes of three southern states were in dispute. Everything depended on the final vote of the electoral college. Garfield was chosen to be one of ten "distinguished Northern visitors" (five from each party) to oversee a recount of votes.

On visiting the South, Garfield was shocked to learn that southern Democrats had forced blacks to vote for the Democratic candidate and terrorized those who tried to hold Republican meetings.

On his return to Washington, Garfield was made a member of an electoral commission that was to decide between Hayes and Tilden.

Republicans squash the Democratic
candidates, Samuel Tilden (right)
and his running mate, Thomas
Hendricks (left).

The Republicans on the commission had to bargain hard
with southern Democrats in order to secure Hayes's peace-
ful inauguration. The result was the Compromise of 1877.
Republicans promised to remove the federal troops that
still remained in the South. They also promised to be fair
to southerners in giving out federal jobs and to vote for
federal funds for improvements in southern states. In
return, southern Democrats agreed to give the election to
Hayes and to deal fairly with blacks.

Rutherford B. Hayes

Garfield had played a key role in the agreements that finally made Rutherford B. Hayes the nineteenth president of the United States. He had the president's complete confidence and admiration. Hayes said of Garfield: "If he were not in public life, he would be equally eminent as a professor in a college, as a lecturer, as an author, an essayist, or a metaphysician." In fact, Hayes urged Garfield to seek the governorship of Ohio as "the surest road to the presidency." Hayes himself had already announced that he would not run again for the highest office.

In 1879, Garfield decided to run for the Senate, even though there were rumors that he could run for president. He noted in his diary: "I have so long and so often seen the evil effects of the presidential fever upon my associates and friends that I am determined it shall not seize upon me." In January 1880, the Ohio legislature elected Garfield to the U.S. Senate.

James A. Garfield had reached the peak of his ambition. When a friend tried to shake his hand in congratulation, Garfield gave him a bear-hug instead, lifting him off the floor and swinging him around in circles. But Garfield was never to take his seat in the Senate.

That summer, at the Republican convention in Chicago, James G. Blaine tried again for the Republican presidential nomination, and Roscoe Conkling tried again to get Grant nominated for a third term.

The hatred between Blaine and Conkling split the Republican party into two factions, one called the Half-Breeds and the other called the Stalwarts. Conkling and his Stalwarts were accusing Blaine and his Half-Breeds of being half-hearted party members.

As head of the Ohio delegation, Garfield avoided taking either side. He nominated his fellow Ohioan, Secretary of the Treasury John Sherman. However, none of the leading candidates could get enough votes.

Someone had nominated Garfield for president, too, but he received only a few votes.

For thirty-three ballots the Stalwarts and the Half-Breeds stalemated each other. Some people feared the convention would end in a riot.

On the thirty-fourth ballot, Wisconsin swung its votes to Garfield. Then Blaine and his Half-Breeds gave Garfield their support. Finally, on the thirty-sixth ballot, James A. Garfield was nominated as the Republican candidate for president. Chester A. Arthur, one of the Stalwarts, was chosen as the vice-presidential candidate in order to please that faction.

Above: The 1880 Republican convention at the Exposition Building in Chicago
Below: A meeting of the National Woman's Suffrage Association at the convention

Lawnfield, the Garfields' farm in Mentor, Ohio

The house in Hiram had been sold, and the Garfields now had a farm in Mentor, Ohio, called Lawnfield. It was from here that Garfield conducted his presidential campaign.

Many groups journeyed by rail to Mentor to pay their respects to the Republican candidate. Garfield personally greeted every group. He would give a little speech and then offer each group light refreshments.

Outside Mentor, though, it was a bitter, hard-fought campaign. The hatred between the Stalwarts and the Half-Breeds continued to grow. But the times were once again prosperous, and though President Hayes was not responsible for this, he and his party received the credit.

The honor of the presidency passes from Hayes (right) to Garfield (left).

Garfield won the popular vote by a slight margin. But by carrying the state of New York, he gained a comfortable majority of the electoral votes. His election to the presidency, unlike Hayes's, was a clear victory.

At this time, Garfield began to have strange nightmares about death, as Lincoln had had before him.

Chapter 7

The Tragic End

As soon as the election results were in, Garfield began to be plagued by office seekers. (One of them, Charles J. Guiteau, he would encounter again.) A wave of letters deluged the new president's desk every day, and long lines of people presented themselves at his doorstep. They even stopped his carriage to ask for jobs. No wonder that, at his inauguration in March 1881, Garfield spoke of the need for civil service to be regulated by law.

Garfield also spoke of the new role of the Negro in American life as "the most important political change . . . since the adoption of the Constitution." He promised to protect the blacks' newly won rights, especially the right to vote.

Garfield's whole family was present for the inauguration, including his eighty-year-old mother. Eliza Garfield was the first mother in American history to see her son inaugurated to the presidency.

The inaugural reception and ball took place that night in the new red brick building of the Smithsonian Institution, which had been completed in time for the event. At the museum, a statue of the Goddess of Liberty held a real electric torch. Few people at that time had ever seen an electric light.

Left: Entitled "At Liberty's Door," this drawing shows Liberty weeping over the deaths of Garfield and Lincoln. The wreath of independence lies on the floor.

Garfield meets with his new cabinet at the White House.

It was fitting that the first use of the museum was for Garfield's inaugural reception. In his approach to science, Garfield was a modern man. As a congressman he had become a link between politics and science, and he made contact with some of the leading scientists of his time.

As president-elect and now president, Garfield had to pick the members of his cabinet, the advisers who would serve him during his term of office. Both Stalwarts and Half-Breeds pressured him to appoint members of their factions. He could not satisfy both sides. Garfield had to fight for his choices, and his victory ultimately caused the downfall of Roscoe Conkling, the Stalwart from New York. Through a bold strike at "boss rule" and the awarding of political jobs, Garfield demonstrated the independence and authority of the presidency.

A cartoon on the Star Route Frauds

During his first four months in office, Garfield faced several heavy trials. In addition to the problem of office seekers and the fight with Conkling, there was a post office scandal.

The Star Route Frauds involved huge amounts of money for delivering mail to thinly populated regions of the West. It was discovered that some of the routes provided no service to anyone. In March 1881, Garfield gave the postmaster general the permission to investigate, though many politicians protested. Six weeks later, the president demanded and received the resignation of Thomas Brady of Indiana, who had been responsible for the Star Route Frauds. This would save the government millions of dollars a year. Garfield's handling of the frauds introduced a new moral tone into the conduct of government.

The Garfields: James, Jr., Mollie, James, mother Eliza, wife Lucretia, and Harry

At the same time, Crete fell seriously ill with malaria. Garfield spent hours at her bedside, helping to nurse her. By July, Crete was out of danger, and Garfield looked forward to a vacation in New England with his family.

With Congress in recess, Garfield planned to travel to Williams College to celebrate the twenty-fifth anniversary of his graduation. He also planned to enroll his sons Harry and Jim in the freshman class at Williams. He left Crete with the other children in Elberon, New Jersey, where it was hoped that the sea air would help Crete to regain her strength. He planned to pick her up in Elberon on his way to New England.

Guiteau fires the second shot, as Blaine looks on in horror.

On the morning of July 2, after a breakfast with James G. Blaine, the two men went to the Baltimore and Potomac railroad station in Washington, where Garfield was to catch the train. Suddenly the sharp crack of a pistol shot rang out, followed by another. The president gasped, "My God! What is this?" and collapsed at Blaine's feet. Harry and Jim, who had been following in another carriage, raced to their father's side and found he had been severely wounded.

The assassin, thirty-nine-year-old Charles J. Guiteau, was a crazed lawyer and office seeker who earlier had bombarded Garfield and Blaine with requests to be made a foreign consul. After shooting Garfield he shouted, "I am a Stalwart! Arthur is now President!"

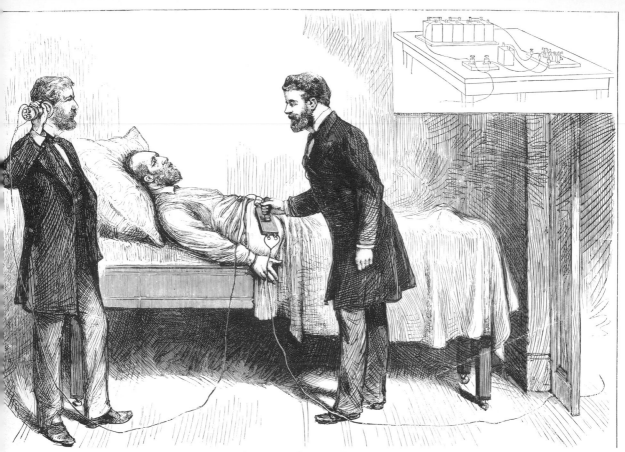

The attempt to locate the bullet in Garfield's body

Guiteau was convinced that he was healing the factional dispute within the Republican party by "removing" Garfield from office. He later revealed that it was Roscoe Conkling's defeat that had inspired him. At his trial, it was established that Guiteau had acted on his own, and he was sentenced to hang for his crime.

For weeks, in the stifling summer heat, Garfield lay between life and death in the White House. The invention of the X ray was fourteen years in the future, and the bullet in his spine could not be located. Alexander Graham Bell, who had invented the telephone, tried to find the bullet with another electrical device that he had invented. Unfortunately for Garfield, it proved unreliable.

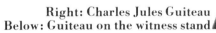
Right: Charles Jules Guiteau
Below: Guiteau on the witness stand

GUITEAU'S FATHER.

Garfield is moved to a train that will take him from Washington to Elberon.

Mollie, now fourteen, wrote in her diary: "We got Papa out of hot Washington, & took him to Elberon, where for the first few days he seemed to rally, but it was merely temporary, & . . . he died at 10:35 p.m. on the 19th of Sept. 1881 . . . oh! it is so hard to lose him; there never was a kinder father, or more devoted & loving husband."

Two months before his fiftieth birthday, James A. Garfield was dead. He had spent two hundred days as chief executive, and for eighty of those days he lay in great pain. Today's X rays, surgery, and antibiotics might have saved his life.

This December 1882 cartoon shows Congress laboring over the civil service reform bill. It shows a stern Santa Claus saying, "Gentlemen, if you don't behave yourselves, you shall not have anything for Christmas."

Eliza Garfield outlived her son by seven years. Crete remained devoted to her husband's memory for thirty-seven years until her death in 1918. Once, when rumors went around that she was marrying again, she replied, proudly, that she certainly was not. "I am the wife of General Garfield," she said.

Garfield's death brought public pressure for civil service reform. In 1883 Congress passed the Pendleton Act, by which a bipartisan Civil Service Commission was established. Only through competitive examinations could many government jobs be obtained. The commission would also protect government workers from dismissal for political reasons.

President James A. Garfield, whose life had been devoted to public service, thus made one last contribution through his tragic death.

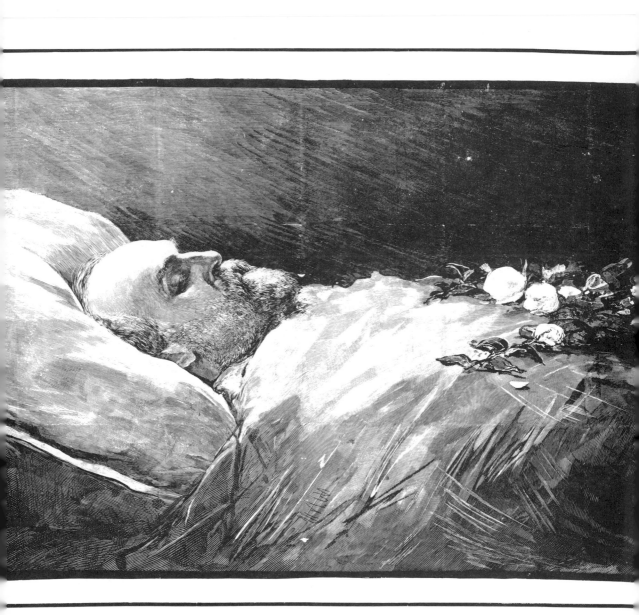

Above: James A. Garfield—born in Orange, Ohio, November 19, 1831; died in Elberon, New Jersey, September 19, 1881

Opposite page: Lady Liberty prays for Garfield's life in this illustrated poem, published in July 1881, two months before the president died.

GOD SAVE THE PRESIDENT!

O LORD of Life, before Thy throne
  Thy sorrowing children bend the knee;
  They lift their fervent prayer to Thee,
For Thou canst save, and Thou alone.

In every clime, in every tongue
  Wherein Thy children learn to pray,
  Rise strong petitions day by day
From hearts with fear and sorrow wrung.

O Fount of Mercy, unrestrained
  Send forth Thy gracious healing power,
  And grant that in this anxious hour
The bitter cup may pass undrained.

Wilt Thou not hear, and hearing grant
  The world's, the stricken nation's plea,
  That all our sorrowing prayers may be
Changed to a glad thanksgiving chant?

Chronology of American History

(Shaded area covers events in James A. Garfield's lifetime.)

About A.D. 982 — Eric the Red, born in Norway, reaches Greenland in one of the first European voyages to North America.

About 985 — Eric the Red brings settlers from Iceland to Greenland.

About 1000 — Leif Ericson (Eric the Red's son) leads what is thought to be the first European expedition to mainland North America; Leif probably lands in Canada.

1492 — Christopher Columbus, seeking a sea route from Spain to the Far East, discovers the New World.

1497 — John Cabot reaches Canada in the first English voyage to North America.

1513 — Ponce de Léon explores Florida in search of the fabled Fountain of Youth.

1519-1521 — Hernando Cortés of Spain conquers Mexico.

1534 — French explorers led by Jacques Cartier enter the Gulf of St. Lawrence in Canada.

1540 — Spanish explorer Francisco Coronado begins exploring the American Southwest, seeking the riches of the mythical Seven Cities of Cibola.

1565 — St. Augustine, Florida, the first permanent European town in what is now the United States, is founded by the Spanish.

1607 — Jamestown, Virginia, is founded, the first permanent English town in the present-day U.S.

1608 — Frenchman Samuel de Champlain founds the village of Quebec, Canada.

1609 — Henry Hudson explores the eastern coast of present-day U.S. for the Netherlands; the Dutch then claim parts of New York, New Jersey, Delaware, and Connecticut and name the area New Netherland.

1619 — The English colonies' first shipment of black slaves arrives in Jamestown.

1620 — English Pilgrims found Massachusetts' first permanent town at Plymouth.

1621 — Massachusetts Pilgrims and Indians hold the famous first Thanksgiving feast in colonial America.

1623 — Colonization of New Hampshire is begun by the English.

1624 — Colonization of present-day New York State is begun by the Dutch at Fort Orange (Albany).

1625 — The Dutch start building New Amsterdam (now New York City).

1630 — The town of Boston, Massachusetts, is founded by the English Puritans.

1633 — Colonization of Connecticut is begun by the English.

1634 — Colonization of Maryland is begun by the English.

1636 — Harvard, the colonies' first college, is founded in Massachusetts. Rhode Island colonization begins when Englishman Roger Williams founds Providence.

1638 — Delaware colonization begins when Swedish people build Fort Christina at present-day Wilmington.

1640 — Stephen Daye of Cambridge, Massachusetts, prints *The Bay Psalm Book*, the first English-language book published in what is now the U.S.

1643 — Swedish settlers begin colonizing Pennsylvania.

About 1650 — North Carolina is colonized by Virginia settlers.

1660 — New Jersey colonization is begun by the Dutch at present-day Jersey City.

1670 — South Carolina colonization is begun by the English near Charleston.

1673 — Jacques Marquette and Louis Jolliet explore the upper Mississippi River for France.

1682—Philadelphia, Pennsylvania, is settled. La Salle explores Mississippi River all the way to its mouth in Louisiana and claims the whole Mississippi Valley for France.

1693—College of William and Mary is founded in Williamsburg, Virginia.

1700—Colonial population is about 250,000.

1703—Benjamin Franklin is born in Boston.

1732—George Washington, first president of the U.S., is born in Westmoreland County, Virginia.

1733—James Oglethorpe founds Savannah, Georgia; Georgia is established as the thirteenth colony.

1735—John Adams, second president of the U.S., is born in Braintree, Massachusetts.

1737—William Byrd founds Richmond, Virginia.

1738—British troops are sent to Georgia over border dispute with Spain.

1739—Black insurrection takes place in South Carolina.

1740—English Parliament passes act allowing naturalization of immigrants to American colonies after seven-year residence.

1743—Thomas Jefferson, third president of the U.S., is born in Albemarle County, Virginia. Benjamin Franklin retires at age thirty-seven to devote himself to scientific inquiries and public service.

1744—King George's War begins; France joins war effort against England.

1745—During King George's War, France raids settlements in Maine and New York.

1747—Classes begin at Princeton College in New Jersey.

1748—The Treaty of Aix-la-Chapelle concludes King George's War.

1749—Parliament legally recognizes slavery in colonies and the inauguration of the plantation system in the South. George Washington becomes the surveyor for Culpepper County in Virginia.

1750—Thomas Walker passes through and names Cumberland Gap on his way toward Kentucky region. Colonial population is about 1,200,000.

1751—James Madison, fourth president of the U.S., is born in Port Conway, Virginia. English Parliament passes Currency Act, banning New England colonies from issuing paper money. George Washington travels to Barbados.

1752—Pennsylvania Hospital, the first general hospital in the colonies, is founded in Philadelphia. Benjamin Franklin uses a kite in a thunderstorm to demonstrate that lightning is a form of electricity.

1753—George Washington delivers command from Virginia Lieutenant Governor Dinwiddie that the French withdraw from the Ohio River Valley; French disregard the demand. Colonial population is about 1,328,000.

1754—French and Indian War begins (extends to Europe as the Seven Years' War). Washington surrenders at Fort Necessity.

1755—French and Indians ambush General Braddock. Washington becomes commander of Virginia troops.

1756—England declares war on France.

1758—James Monroe, fifth president of the U.S., is born in Westmoreland County, Virginia.

1759—Cherokee Indian war begins in southern colonies; hostilities extend to 1761. George Washington marries Martha Dandridge Custis.

1760—George III becomes king of England. Colonial population is about 1,600,000.

1762—England declares war on Spain.

1763—Treaty of Paris concludes the French and Indian War and the Seven Years' War. England gains Canada and most other French lands east of the Mississippi River.

1764—British pass the Sugar Act to gain tax money from the colonists. The issue of taxation without representation is first introduced in Boston. John Adams marries Abigail Smith.

1765—Stamp Act goes into effect in the colonies. Business virtually stops as almost all colonists refuse to use the stamps.

1766—British repeal the Stamp Act.

1767—John Quincy Adams, sixth president of the U.S. and son of second president John Adams, is born in Braintree, Massachusetts. Andrew Jackson, seventh president of the U.S., is born in Waxhaw settlement, South Carolina.

1769—Daniel Boone sights the Kentucky Territory.

1770—In the Boston Massacre, British soldiers kill five colonists and injure six. Townshend Acts are repealed, thus eliminating all duties on imports to the colonies except tea.

1771—Benjamin Franklin begins his autobiography, a work that he will never complete. The North Carolina assembly passes the "Bloody Act," which makes rioters guilty of treason.

1772—Samuel Adams rouses colonists to consider British threats to self-government. Thomas Jefferson marries Martha Wayles Skelton.

1773—English Parliament passes the Tea Act. Colonists dressed as Mohawk Indians board British tea ships and toss 342 casks of tea into the water in what becomes known as the Boston Tea Party. William Henry Harrison is born in Charles City County, Virginia.

1774—British close the port of Boston to punish the city for the Boston Tea Party. First Continental Congress convenes in Philadelphia.

1775—American Revolution begins with battles of Lexington and Concord, Massachusetts. Second Continental Congress opens in Philadelphia. George Washington becomes commander-in-chief of the Continental army.

1776—Declaration of Independence is adopted on July 4.

1777—Congress adopts the American flag with thirteen stars and thirteen stripes. John Adams is sent to France to negotiate peace treaty.

1778—France declares war against Great Britain and becomes U.S. ally.

1779—British surrender to Americans at Vincennes. Thomas Jefferson is elected governor of Virginia. James Madison is elected to the Continental Congress.

1780—Benedict Arnold, first American traitor, defects to the British.

1781—Articles of Confederation go into effect. Cornwallis surrenders to George Washington at Yorktown, ending the American Revolution.

1782—American commissioners, including John Adams, sign peace treaty with British in Paris. Thomas Jefferson's wife, Martha, dies. Martin Van Buren is born in Kinderhook, New York.

1784—Zachary Taylor is born near Barboursville, Virginia.

1785—Congress adopts the dollar as the unit of currency. John Adams is made minister to Great Britain. Thomas Jefferson is appointed minister to France.

1786—Shays' Rebellion begins in Massachusetts.

1787—Constitutional Convention assembles in Philadelphia, with George Washington presiding; U.S. Constitution is adopted. Delaware, New Jersey, and Pennsylvania become states.

1788—Virginia, South Carolina, New York, Connecticut, New Hampshire, Maryland, and Massachusetts become states. U.S. Constitution is ratified. New York City is declared U.S. capital.

1789—Presidential electors elect George Washington and John Adams as first president and vice-president. Thomas Jefferson is appointed secretary of state. North Carolina becomes a state. French Revolution begins.

1790—Supreme Court meets for the first time. Rhode Island becomes a state. First national census in the U.S. counts 3,929,214 persons. John Tyler is born in Charles City County, Virginia.

1791—Vermont enters the Union. U.S. Bill of Rights, the first ten amendments to the Constitution, goes into effect. District of Columbia is established.

1792—Thomas Paine publishes *The Rights of Man*. Kentucky becomes a state. Two political parties are formed in the U.S., Federalist and Republican. Washington is elected to a second term, with Adams as vice-president.

1793—War between France and Britain begins; U.S. declares neutrality. Eli Whitney invents the cotton gin; cotton production and slave labor increase in the South.

1794—Eleventh Amendment to the Constitution is passed, limiting federal courts' power. "Whiskey Rebellion" in Pennsylvania protests federal whiskey tax. James Madison marries Dolley Payne Todd.

1795—George Washington signs the Jay Treaty with Great Britain. Treaty of San Lorenzo, between U.S. and Spain, settles Florida boundary and gives U.S. right to navigate the Mississippi. James Polk is born near Pineville, North Carolina.

1796—Tennessee enters the Union. Washington gives his Farewell Address, refusing a third presidential term. John Adams is elected president and Thomas Jefferson vice-president.

1797—Adams recommends defense measures against possible war with France. Napoleon Bonaparte and his army march against Austrians in Italy. U.S. population is about 4,900,000.

1798—Washington is named commander-in-chief of the U.S. army. Department of the Navy is created. Alien and Sedition Acts are passed. Napoleon's troops invade Egypt and Switzerland.

1799—George Washington dies at Mount Vernon. James Monroe is elected governor of Virginia. French Revolution ends. Napoleon becomes ruler of France.

1800—Thomas Jefferson and Aaron Burr tie for president. U.S. capital is moved from Philadelphia to Washington, D.C. The White House is built as presidents' home. Spain returns Louisiana to France. Millard Fillmore is born in Locke, New York.

1801—After thirty-six ballots, House of Representatives elects Thomas Jefferson president, making Burr vice-president. James Madison is named secretary of state.

1802—Congress abolishes excise taxes. U.S. Military Academy is founded at West Point, New York.

1803—Ohio enters the Union. Louisiana Purchase treaty is signed with France, greatly expanding U.S. territory.

1804—Twelfth Amendment to the Constitution rules that president and vice-president be elected separately. Alexander Hamilton is killed by Vice-President Aaron Burr in a duel. Orleans Territory is established. Napoleon crowns himself emperor of France.

1805—Thomas Jefferson begins his second term as president. Lewis and Clark expedition reaches the Pacific Ocean.

1806—Coinage of silver dollars is stopped; resumes in 1836.

1807—Aaron Burr is acquitted in treason trial. Embargo Act closes U.S. ports to trade.

1808—James Madison is elected president. Congress outlaws importing slaves from Africa.

1810—U.S. population is 7,240,000.

1811—William Henry Harrison defeats Indians at Tippecanoe. Monroe is named secretary of state.

1812—Louisiana becomes a state. U.S. declares war on Britain (War of 1812). James Madison is reelected president. Napoleon invades Russia.

1813—British forces take Fort Niagara and Buffalo, New York.

1814—Francis Scott Key writes "The Star-Spangled Banner." British troops burn much of Washington, D.C., including the White House. Treaty of Ghent ends War of 1812. James Monroe becomes secretary of war.

1815—Napoleon meets his final defeat at Battle of Waterloo.

1816—James Monroe is elected president. Indiana becomes a state.

1817—Mississippi becomes a state. Construction on Erie Canal begins.

1818—Illinois enters the Union. The present thirteen-stripe flag is adopted. Border between U.S. and Canada is agreed upon.

1819—Alabama becomes a state. U.S. purchases Florida from Spain. Thomas Jefferson establishes the University of Virginia.

1820—James Monroe is reelected. In the Missouri Compromise, Maine enters the Union as a free (non-slave) state.

1821—Missouri enters the Union as a slave state. Santa Fe Trail opens the American Southwest. Mexico declares independence from Spain. Napoleon Bonaparte dies.

1822—U.S. recognizes Mexico and Colombia. Liberia in Africa is founded as a home for freed slaves.

1823—Monroe Doctrine closes North and South America to European colonizing or invasion.

1824—House of Representatives elects John Quincy Adams president when none of the four candidates wins a majority in national election. Mexico becomes a republic.

1825—Erie Canal is opened. U.S. population is 11,300,000.

1826—Thomas Jefferson and John Adams both die on July 4, the fiftieth anniversary of the Declaration of Independence.

1828—Andrew Jackson is elected president. Tariff of Abominations is passed, cutting imports.

1829—James Madison attends Virginia's constitutional convention. Slavery is abolished in Mexico.

1830—Indian Removal Act to resettle Indians west of the Mississippi is approved.

1831—James Monroe dies in New York City. James A. Garfield is born in Orange, Ohio. Cyrus McCormick develops his reaper.

1832—Andrew Jackson, nominated by the new Democratic Party, is reelected president.

1833—Britain abolishes slavery in its colonies.

1835—Federal government becomes debt-free for the first time.

1836—Martin Van Buren becomes president. Texas wins independence from Mexico. Arkansas joins the Union. James Madison dies at Montpelier, Virginia.

1837—Michigan enters the Union. U.S. population is 15,900,000.

1840—William Henry Harrison is elected president.

1841—President Harrison dies in Washington, D.C., one month after inauguration. Vice-President John Tyler succeeds him.

1844—James Knox Polk is elected president. Samuel Morse sends first telegraphic message.

1845—Texas and Florida become states. Potato famine in Ireland causes massive emigration from Ireland to U.S. Andrew Jackson dies near Nashville, Tennessee.

1846—Iowa enters the Union. War with Mexico begins.

1847—U.S. captures Mexico City.

1848—Zachary Taylor becomes president. Treaty of Guadalupe Hidalgo ends Mexico-U.S. war. Wisconsin becomes a state.

1849—James Polk dies in Nashville, Tennessee.

1850—President Taylor dies in Washington, D.C.; Vice-President Millard Fillmore succeeds him. California enters the Union, breaking tie between slave and free states.

1852—Franklin Pierce is elected president.

1853—Gadsden Purchase transfers Mexican territory to U.S.

1854—"War for Bleeding Kansas" is fought between slave and free states.

1855—Czar Nicholas I of Russia dies, succeeded by Alexander II.

1856—James Buchanan is elected president. In Massacre of Potawatomi Creek, Kansas-slavers are murdered by free-staters.

1858—Minnesota enters the Union. Theodore Roosevelt is born in New York City.

1859—Oregon becomes a state.

1860—Abraham Lincoln is elected president; South Carolina secedes from the Union in protest.

1861—Arkansas, Tennessee, North Carolina, and Virginia secede. Kansas enters the Union as a free state. Civil War begins.

1862—Union forces capture Fort Henry, Roanoke Island, Fort Donelson, Jacksonville, and New Orleans; Union armies are defeated at the battles of Bull Run and Fredericksburg. Martin Van Buren dies in Kinderhook, New York. John Tyler dies near Charles City, Virginia.

1863—Lincoln issues Emancipation Proclamation: all slaves held in rebelling territories are declared free. West Virginia becomes a state.

1864—Abraham Lincoln is reelected. Nevada becomes a state.

1865—Lincoln is assassinated, succeeded by Andrew Johnson. U.S. Civil War ends on May 26. Thirteenth Amendment abolishes slavery.

1867—Nebraska becomes a state. U.S. buys Alaska from Russia for $7,200,000. Reconstruction Acts are passed.

1868—President Johnson is impeached for violating Tenure of Office Act, but is acquitted by Senate. Ulysses S. Grant is elected president. Fourteenth Amendment prohibits voting discrimination.

1870—Fifteenth Amendment gives blacks the right to vote.

1872—Grant is reelected over Horace Greeley. General Amnesty Act pardons ex-Confederates.

1874—Millard Fillmore dies in Buffalo, New York. Herbert Hoover is born in West Branch, Iowa.

1876—Colorado enters the Union. "Custer's last stand": he and his men are massacred by Sioux Indians at Little Big Horn, Montana.

1877—Rutherford B. Hayes is elected president as all disputed votes are awarded to him.

1880—James A. Garfield is elected president.

1881—President Garfield is assassinated and dies in Elberon, New Jersey. Vice-President Chester A. Arthur succeeds him.

1882—U.S. bans Chinese immigration. Franklin D. Roosevelt is born in Hyde Park, New York.

1884—Grover Cleveland is elected president.

1886—Statue of Liberty is dedicated.

1888—Benjamin Harrison is elected president.

1889—North Dakota, South Dakota, Washington, and Montana become states.

1890—Dwight D. Eisenhower is born in Denison, Texas. Idaho and Wyoming become states.

1892—Grover Cleveland is elected president.

1896—William McKinley is elected president. Utah becomes a state.

1898—U.S. declares war on Spain over Cuba.

1900—McKinley is reelected. Boxer Rebellion against foreigners in China begins.

1901—McKinley is assassinated by anarchist; he is succeeded by Theodore Roosevelt.

1902—U.S. acquires perpetual control over Panama Canal.

1903—Alaskan frontier is settled.

1904—Russian-Japanese War breaks out. Theodore Roosevelt wins presidential election.

1905—Treaty of Portsmouth signed, ending Russian-Japanese War.

1906—U.S. troops occupy Cuba.

1907—President Roosevelt bars all Japanese immigration. Oklahoma enters the Union.

1908—William Howard Taft becomes president. Lyndon B. Johnson is born near Stonewall, Texas.

1909—NAACP is founded under W.E.B. DuBois

1910—China abolishes slavery.

1911—Chinese Revolution begins.

1912—Woodrow Wilson is elected president. Arizona and New Mexico become states.

1913—Federal income tax is introduced in U.S. through the Sixteenth Amendment. Richard Nixon is born in Yorba Linda, California.

1914—World War I begins.

1915—British liner *Lusitania* is sunk by German submarine.

1916—Wilson is reelected president.

1917—U.S. breaks diplomatic relations with Germany. Czar Nicholas of Russia abdicates as revolution begins. U.S. declares war on Austria-Hungary. John F. Kennedy is born in Brookline, Massachusetts.

1918—Wilson proclaims "Fourteen Points" as war aims. On November 11, armistice is signed between Allies and Germany.

1919—Eighteenth Amendment prohibits sale and manufacture of intoxicating liquors. Wilson presides over first League of Nations; wins Nobel Peace Prize. Theodore Roosevelt dies in Oyster Bay, New York.

1920—Nineteenth Amendment (women's suffrage) is passed. Warren Harding is elected president.

1921—Adolf Hitler's stormtroopers begin to terrorize political opponents.

1922—Irish Free State is established. Soviet states form USSR. Benito Mussolini forms Fascist government in Italy.

1923—President Harding dies; he is succeeded by Vice-President Calvin Coolidge.

1924—Coolidge is elected president.

1925—Hitler reorganizes Nazi Party and publishes first volume of *Mein Kampf.*

1926—Fascist youth organizations founded in Germany and Italy. Republic of Lebanon proclaimed.

1927—Stalin becomes Soviet dictator. Economic conference in Geneva attended by fifty-two nations.

1928—Herbert Hoover is elected president. U.S. and many other nations sign Kellogg-Briand pacts to outlaw war.

1929—Stock prices in New York crash on "Black Thursday"; the Great Depression begins.

1930—Bank of U.S. and its many branches close (most significant bank failure of the year).

1931—Emigration from U.S. exceeds immigration for first time as Depression deepens.

1932—Franklin D. Roosevelt wins presidential election in a Democratic landslide.

1933—First concentration camps are erected in Germany. U.S. recognizes USSR and resumes trade. Twenty-First Amendment repeals prohibition.

1934—Severe dust storms hit Plains states. President Roosevelt passes U.S. Social Security Act.

1936—Roosevelt is reelected. Spanish Civil War begins. Hitler and Mussolini form Rome-Berlin Axis.

1937—Roosevelt signs Neutrality Act.

1938—Roosevelt sends appeal to Hitler and Mussolini to settle European problems amicably.

1939—Germany takes over Czechoslovakia and invades Poland, starting World War II.

1940—Roosevelt is reelected for a third term.

1941—Japan bombs Pearl Harbor, U.S. declares war on Japan. Germany and Italy declare war on U.S.; U.S. then declares war on them.

1942—Allies agree not to make separate peace treaties with the enemies. U.S. government transfers more than 100,000 Nisei (Japanese-Americans) from west coast to inland concentration camps.

1943—Allied bombings of Germany begin.

1944—Roosevelt is reelected for a fourth term. Allied forces invade Normandy on D-Day.

1945—President Franklin D. Roosevelt dies in Warm Springs, Georgia; Vice-President Harry S. Truman succeeds him. Mussolini is killed; Hitler commits suicide. Germany surrenders. U.S. drops atomic bomb on Hiroshima; Japan surrenders; end of World War II.

1946—U.N. General Assembly holds its first session in London. Peace conference of twenty-one nations is held in Paris.

1947—Peace treaties are signed in Paris. "Cold War" is in full swing.

1948—U.S. passes Marshall Plan Act, providing $17 billion in aid for Europe. U.S. recognizes new nation of Israel. India and Pakistan become free of British rule. Truman is elected president.

1949—Republic of Eire is proclaimed in Dublin. Russia blocks land route access from Western Germany to Berlin; airlift begins. U.S., France, and Britain agree to merge their zones of occupation in West Germany. Apartheid program begins in South Africa.

1950—Riots in Johannesburg, South Africa, against apartheid. North Korea invades South Korea. U.N. forces land in South Korea and recapture Seoul.

1951—Twenty-Second Amendment limits president to two terms.

1952—Dwight D. Eisenhower resigns as supreme commander in Europe and is elected president.

1953—Stalin dies; struggle for power in Russia follows. Rosenbergs are executed for espionage.

1954—U.S. and Japan sign mutual defense agreement.

1955—Blacks in Montgomery, Alabama, boycott segregated bus lines.

1956—Eisenhower is reelected president. Soviet troops march into Hungary.

1957—U.S. agrees to withdraw ground forces from Japan. Russia launches first satellite, *Sputnik*.

1958—European Common Market comes into being. Alaska becomes the forty-ninth state. Fidel Castro begins war against Batista government in Cuba.

1959—Hawaii becomes fiftieth state. Castro becomes premier of Cuba. De Gaulle is proclaimed president of the Fifth Republic of France.

1960—Historic debates between Senator John F. Kennedy and Vice-President Richard Nixon are televised. Kennedy is elected president. Brezhnev becomes president of USSR.

1961—Berlin Wall is constructed. Kennedy and Khrushchev confer in Vienna. In Bay of Pigs incident, Cubans trained by CIA attempt to overthrow Castro.

1962—U.S. military council is established in South Vietnam.

1963—Riots and beatings by police and whites mark civil rights demonstrations in Birmingham, Alabama; 30,000 troops are called out. Martin Luther King, Jr., is arrested. Freedom marchers descend on Washington, D.C., to demonstrate. President Kennedy is assassinated in Dallas, Texas; Vice-President Lyndon B. Johnson is sworn in as president.

1964—U.S. aircraft bomb North Vietnam. Johnson is elected president. Herbert Hoover dies in New York City.

1965—U.S. combat troops arrive in South Vietnam.

1966—Thousands protest U.S. policy in Vietnam. National Guard quells race riots in Chicago.

1967—Six-Day War between Israel and Arab nations.

1968—Martin Luther King, Jr., is assassinated in Memphis, Tennessee. Senator Robert Kennedy is assassinated in Los Angeles. Riots and police brutality take place at Democratic National Convention in Chicago. Richard Nixon is elected president. Czechoslovakia is invaded by Soviet troops.

1969—Dwight D. Eisenhower dies in Washington, D.C. Hundreds of thousands of people in several U.S. cities demonstrate against Vietnam War.

1970 — Four Vietnam War protesters are killed by National Guardsmen at Kent State University in Ohio.

1971 — Twenty-Sixth Amendment allows eighteen-year-olds to vote.

1972 — Nixon visits Communist China; is reelected president in near-record landslide. Watergate affair begins when five men are arrested in the Watergate hotel complex in Washington, D.C. Nixon announces resignations of aides Haldeman, Ehrlichman, and Dean and Attorney General Kleindienst as a result of Watergate-related charges. Harry S. Truman dies in Kansas City, Missouri.

1973 — Vice-President Spiro Agnew resigns; Gerald Ford is named vice-president. Vietnam peace treaty is formally approved after nineteen months of negotiations. Lyndon B. Johnson dies in San Antonio, Texas.

1974 — As a result of Watergate cover-up, impeachment is considered; Nixon resigns and Ford becomes president. Ford pardons Nixon and grants limited amnesty to Vietnam War draft evaders and military deserters.

1975 — U.S. civilians are evacuated from Saigon, South Vietnam, as Communist forces complete takeover of South Vietnam.

1976 — U.S. celebrates its Bicentennial. James Earl Carter becomes president.

1977 — Carter pardons most Vietnam draft evaders, numbering some 10,000.

1980 — Ronald Reagan is elected president.

1981 — President Reagan is shot in the chest in assassination attempt. Sandra Day O'Connor is appointed first woman justice of the Supreme Court.

1983 — U.S. troops invade island of Grenada.

1984 — Reagan is reelected president. Democratic candidate Walter Mondale's running mate, Geraldine Ferraro, is the first woman selected for vice-president by a major U.S. political party.

1985 — Soviet Communist Party secretary Konstantin Chernenko dies; Mikhail Gorbachev succeeds him. U.S. and Soviet officials discuss arms control in Geneva. Reagan and Gorbachev hold summit conference in Geneva. Racial tensions accelerate in South Africa.

1986 — Space shuttle *Challenger* explodes shortly after takeoff; crew of seven dies. U.S. bombs bases in Libya. Corazon Aquino defeats Ferdinand Marcos in Philippine presidential election.

1987 — Iraqi missile rips the U.S. frigate *Stark* in the Persian Gulf, killing thirty-seven American sailors. Congress holds hearings to investigate sale of U.S. arms to Iran to finance Nicaraguan *contra* movement.

1988 — George Bush is elected president. President Reagan and Soviet leader Gorbachev sign INF treaty, eliminating intermediate nuclear forces. Severe drought sweeps the United States.

Index

Page numbers in boldface type indicate illustrations.

About the Author

Dee Lillegard is the author of *September To September, Poems for All Year Round*, a teacher resource, and many easy readers, including titles for Childrens Press's *I Can Be* career series. For the *Encyclopedia of Presidents* series, she has written biographies of John Tyler, James K. Polk, James A. Garfield, and Richard Nixon. Over two hundred of Ms. Lillegard's stories, poems, and puzzles have appeared in numerous children's magazines. Ms. Lillegard lives in the San Francisco Bay Area, where she teaches Writing for Children.